The Mirror Love

To the young man whose presence ignited the spark
of my passion for writing.

It is to you, dear soul, that I dedicate these heartfelt
verses, woven from the threads of gratitude and
reverence. Your gentle guidance led me through the
labyrinth of my emotions, inspiring me to delve
deep into the recesses of my soul and lay bare the
raw essence of my being upon the page.

I am eternally grateful for our encounter, for it was
your presence that I learned the true meaning of
unconditional love. Thank you for being the light
that illuminated my path, guiding me towards a love
that knows no bounds.

Contents

Introduction

I became entangled with another soul in the depths of my existence, amidst the turbulent waves of my experience; it was a profound and thrilling connection. However, it was an untimely bond that neither of us was ready to accept.

In 2020, when I set out on my spiritual journey, I came upon this individual—a reflection of my own unresolved issues and open wounds. I made my way through the maze of feelings as I explored my identity, including infatuation, despair, tension, jealousy, rage, frustration, loneliness, and yes, love.

So, to all who read these words, I implore you: love yourself fiercely and relentlessly, even when the world refuses to reciprocate. For within you lies a power beyond measure, a worthiness that transcends the fleeting affections of others.

This poem is for the ones who have walked the path of love but ended up standing by themselves at its edge, struggling with feelings that have been revealed and weaknesses that have been exposed. It is for people who have gone through the same thing as me.

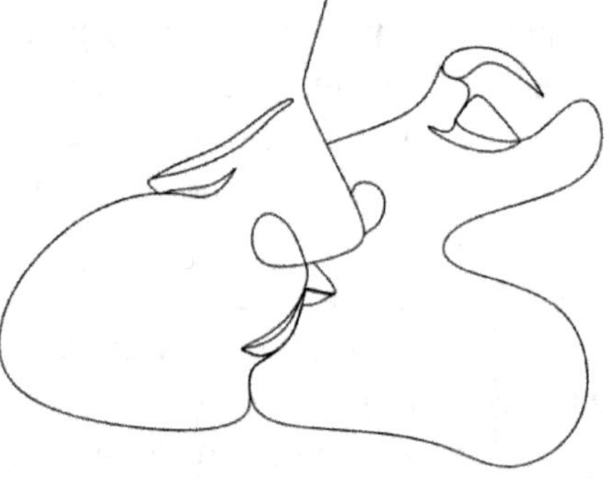

First poem I wrote

I love you, but I don't know why.
The moment I met you I knew it was you.
No, I am lying I didn't not have a clue
I am too indecisive. I do not know which is
true.
But the moment you came back in my dream
 I knew something was new
I know I cannot be with you.
But in my dreams, I remember you
Not in this life not who you are or your name
None of it was the same.
Sometimes I am confused, and I go blank.
I am not good with things like this
But I am asking myself what did I miss?
I wonder what it would feel like if I had just one
kiss.

Had to lose sight of you

It did no good trying to erase you,
Instead of trying to embrace you.
You are not the problem, it is also me,
This dynamic is hard.
It is not like I can give up and leave,
I am also learning not to give up on myself.
It can be lonely not being able to ask for help,
Many days, I think of you and start to weep.
I know your purpose is for growth,
But the pain is too much, it is loath.

Past, Present and Future

You have mentioned my past.

With your presence,

Showing so much absence.

In the future,

I will forever be transformed.

Through this insight,

You shine a light on different areas.

I had to heal.

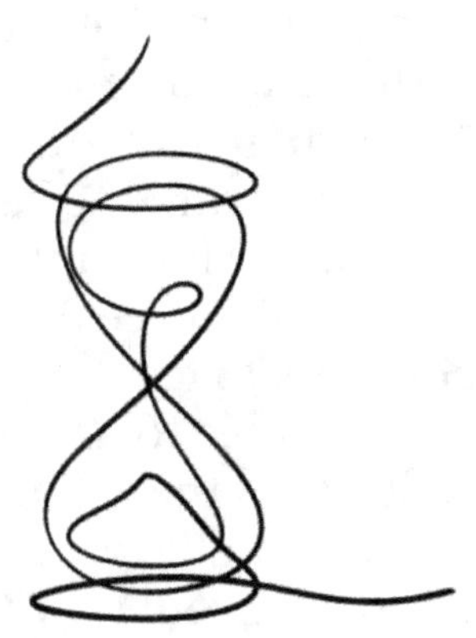

Finding You

You were the best thing I discovered.
A connection that I hold dear to my heart.
You unearthed the feelings I tried to cover.
I knew when I liked you; there was something
there from the start.
I was always scared to call you, my lover.
You do not know how much I admire you, my
favorite piece of God's art.
You enabled me to feel things I have never been
able to uncover.
I should let go of these thoughts, because that
would be very smart.
I found love in you; now I need to find it in
me.
I hope one day it will be true when they say we
were meant to be.

To the half that can see me.

Your light truly shines through.

The Sacred Kiss

You kept giving me this look, as if you were talking
with your eyes.
I become weak for you every single time.
Venus in Pisces, I would fall for all your lies.
I love connecting to you as if you are mine.
It is like we are stuck together; we have this special
tie.
I fell too deep and really lost myself inside.
Wanting to make you happy was all I tried every
time.
I wanted to pull away, but I came in closer.
By the time you looked at me, I was extremely shy.
So close together, you secretly gave me a kiss on the
cheek.
That made me fully awake.
The energy was so powerful;
I felt the whole thing radiate through my body.
Like an earthquake.
The kiss was so intense;
I wish it could happen again.
But I am back in reality,
Must come to my common sense.
Now this was something that happened in a dream.
I wish I could go back in time just for this one
glimpse.
Letting it go is the best thing now,
But it will always be there, the feeling recorded in
my body.

I could never forget the touch.

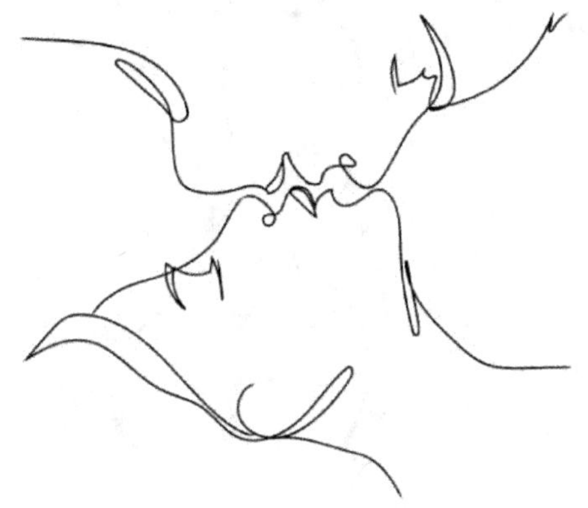

Lost in Lust

Lost in lust, reality fades to dust.
I should not want you, yet I crave your touch.
But the truth is, I am lost, yearning too much.

Each day, desire burns, reason fails,
Your presence is a fire, igniting love's sails.
Yet I know the risk, heartache's harsh trails,
But I am drawn to you, as desperation prevails.

The back and Forth

You are not in my presence; this isn't anything
new.
It was me consistently manifesting a ridiculous
dude.
I am not trying to disrespect you; it is more of
my fault.
I fantasize a version of you I thought would
come true.
The crazy part about is that I have no clue that
it's truly you.

I cannot let you hurt me again.

If you are me, and I am you,
This is the broken version.
I am ready to see the other side,
We have been on this side for so long.
One part is numb, and the other wants to move
on.
I need to go back into my cocoon so I can
re-blossom,
I am missing parts of my wings.
I will always remember the transformation you
ignited,
Until then, we must move on; it is only right.
This is for me to decide.
Because I am choosing to love in this life.

If we are truly connected, you will reappear
when it is right.

To my darling

I cannot hold you.

I held you so tightly.

I feared to let you go.

Attached to my mind, body, and soul

The fear of releasing you.

When it should have been losing me

How awful should I be?

Learning to love myself

Knowing it does not end

All that I have left is me.

Time to grow new seeds.

Following the Crowd

You follow the crowd as if you are part of the
click of a crow.

Little do you know that the knowledge God
gave you holds so much power. You were put
on Earth to teach others about your growth.

Yes, leader, I claim you to be

But you must leave all of what you thought you
needed behind.

Family, friends, and things that are hindering
you

Let God work through you, it will be about time
to surrender soon.

Remember why you are here!

It's not the materialistic or tangible things

You were here to ascend and learn
unconditional love.

Rushing Love

Slow down,

You run through my mind.

Like we are out of time.

Little do you know, we just started

This journey, this dance, uncharted.

In your presence, time bends and sways,

Moments linger, in a blissful haze.

But let us not rush, let us savor each part,

For in the stillness, we will find our heart.

With every step, let us take our time,

Let us unravel the mysteries, line by line.

For the beauty lies not in the end,

It's about having sacred moments on the journey, my friend.

Perfect you

Your smile is gracious.

Do not change it.

Take time and learn to embrace it.

Find a way to love all the spaces.

The crookedness is unique. Stop critiquing.

Everything about you is extremely unique.

&

Stop letting people control you.

Those types of people will makc you go back to
the old you.

Embrace your power, let your authenticity
shine,

In reclaiming yourself, you will find true
liberation.

Be You I like U

I love your light and your dark parts.

I love your ups and your downs.

I can tell you are a fighter.

Because you are still around.

I know how bad that might sound.

But the understanding of it is profound.

You keep showing up in the world, knowing
what you are going through.

May God give you strength.

To keep pulling through

I watch and see you grow.

You plant a new seed everywhere you go.

Have thoughts of giving up?

But no, it is too late.

As you turn around for a second,

Things are starting to process, and it looks
great.

If you stare too long, you will forget what is in
front of you.

{Continue to pray God is guiding you}

Unique Love will find you

Love is on the horizon.

Hate is what they try to get you disguised in.

Love is what you want. Quit trying to deny it.

Self-hatred is what they teach, but deep down,
you know that is not right.

What you hold on to is deceit.

Self-love is the best love. Take it from someone
who is learning it.

It is something that you must go through.

You understand you must rebuild the bridge
you once knew, burn it first, then understand,
remake, and relearn it.

Self-sabotage to lose touch of you

I am debating whether the love that I feel for
myself up with if it is good or bad.

Because lots of times I am holding on to things
that I know will make me sad.

When I get a euphoric feeling, I start to believe
this is only the beginning.

I start to overthink, and my mind goes
completely spinning.

& then the bipolar kicks in, and I start to get
mad.

On my journey, I have learned a lot about how
much I self-sabotage. This poem is to bring
awareness to it. Remember, you can break
these bad habits with awareness and alchemy.
Writing helps me express this and push
towards a more positive attitude.

Once I saw you, I adored you

Once upon a time, I met you.

I saw you walk past my eyes; they were stuck
like glue.

I was extremely curious as to why I was drawn
to you, but I certainly did not have a clue.

Your energy is very radiant.

Your smile should be adored.

The presence you carry should never be
ignored.

Seeing you walk by day to day

It is amazing to watch you. What can I say?

It seems like a simple word to say, hey.

It should never be too hard, but I do not want
to come off as extremely gay.

So radical thoughts could never stay in place.

The open eyes

How can you know what is going on?

But tell no one what is happening.

Because I already did; once again, they started
laughing.

It is like the boy who cried wolf, but this time
around, there was no lie and there never was.

People simply do not care and fall in love with
the material just because.

The sad part is that it is all an illusion.

Just like a game,

We are the players behind the username.

I am sad thinking about how we cannot come
together and realize what is in front of our
eyes.

We are too blinded by the fake, and we see it as
real even though it is blocking us from the
truth in disguise.

I am learning to understand

I cannot control who you are or what you
desire.

I just wish I could be there to support you
through the wire

Discomfort, hurt and pain.

I just never want you to feel as if you are going
insane.

I love you the way you are, and I wish I could
express how that will always remain.

F is For

F is forgetting the past.

You are holding onto it, won't last.

Because your soul will seek more, and your
mind will keep you restrained.

Don't let that be the reason you're holding on
to the pain.

Love is a feeling nurtured by care.

A foundation to keep you whole and aware.

Learn to embrace it, and let it guide your way,

In its depths, you'll find treasures every day.

Ego Neglect

*Rejection
can hurt*

*Makes you
wonder
what your
worth*

*Ego
shattered
thrown
through the
fort*

*Pushed
aside*

*Taught
never
meant to
be heard*

*The pain in which this was taught never
meant to be learned.*

Mad mind

Forget fears.

Release them.

Open your heart.

And be guided by love.

I believe in you.

Close your eyes.

You will see me.

Open them, but you forget what we hold.

I love you.

You're scared of love.

You're scared of me.

I'm the other half of you that you must face.

Our reflection holds codes.

Follow each trace.

Illuminate the light

You never dim the light.

Every time I see you, it's like we connect on-site.

The energy never lies, and the love we hold from within is so bright.

We must push through the dark night.

It's not going to be easy, but it will be alright.

Duality we are just like black and white.

In love w you

I just might.

Deeply in Love

Love is a word to convey what's real.

Yet will I find the courage to reveal?

My feelings in mind.

But in expressing them, I delay.

Impatient, I yearn for you, yet I understand.

Time is needed for you to take my hand.

I'll wait, and whenever you're ready, I'll be there.

Patiently, with love and care.

In my heart, there's only room for you.

No other soul will ever do.

Bitter Sweet

I can't wait any longer, my mind says.

The heart wants what it wants, in its own way.

My soul urges patience, a quiet refrain,

Though our shared moment, though brief,
remains.

It lingers as the longest memory in my mind.

Will we ever share that again, intertwined?

My angels whisper, "Eventually," they decree,

But loneliness settles in when you're not with
me.

I sit here, wondering, as I write,

Will you ever surrender to your heart's delight?

Still, I hold onto the belief that you're drawing
near; it's true.

In my soul, I feel it- a bright spark of
excitement.

Hope arrives- no more stress, only light.

I write to ease my mind.

Missing you deeply, the ache prolonged.

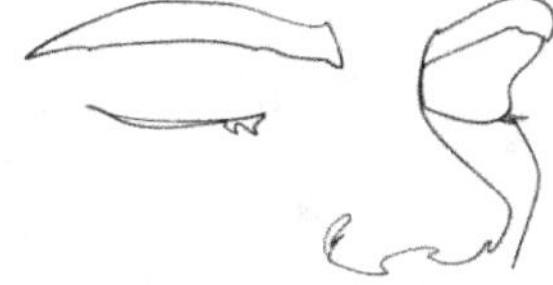

Thoughts

Racing and pacing for you,

I am losing track of what's important; my mind is
blind to anything but you.

I can't seem to think straight, but it seems too late.

A toxic relationship pinpoints life's strife,

I'd rather throw it away than be your potential wife.

Traveling by land and sea,

Cutting up food for you while watching the
beautiful bees.

The imagination I hold for you is quite scary.

I tend not to worry.

Because it's only what I feel and think,

Not like any of this will happen, at least not in a
blink.

If it did, then manifestation is true.

But in this life, I would be genuinely happy simply
with you.

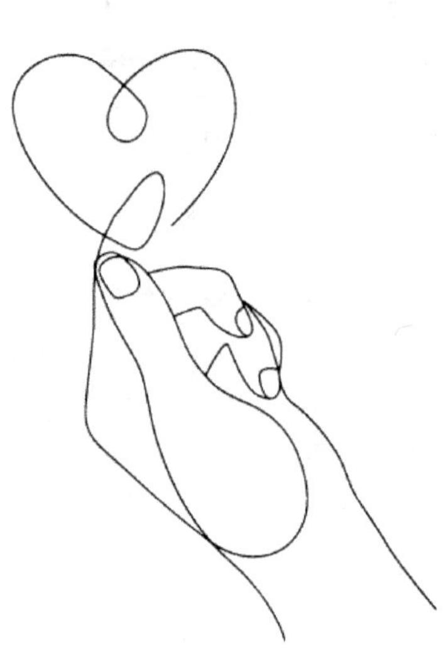

Brown Sugar

Your skin is healthy and beautiful brown, with a little sweetness.

Eyes so precious, one look, and I could go helpless, not wanting anyone to save me from what I feel. Somehow, this is satisfying.

The voice of yours, so raspy and chilling,

Low tone, calm, and soothing- oh, how unique it is.

The smile you have will never grow old.

So nice and lovely, just as your teeth start to shine, I fall in love all over again every single time.

Yin Yan equals 8

Even in the physical, we have a connection.

The special bond between two souls is
affection.

The dynamic is strong; our DNA holds many
codes.

Remembering me is remembering you; our
paths cross.

The eyes, when looked inside, reveal many
clues.

 This connection is so cool; we don't need
words, just cues.

Telepathically, I can sense the muse.

Place your hand on your heart; I'll feel it and
know it's you.

Deep love never needs understanding; the
heart knows what to do.

Our love frequency holds a special hue.

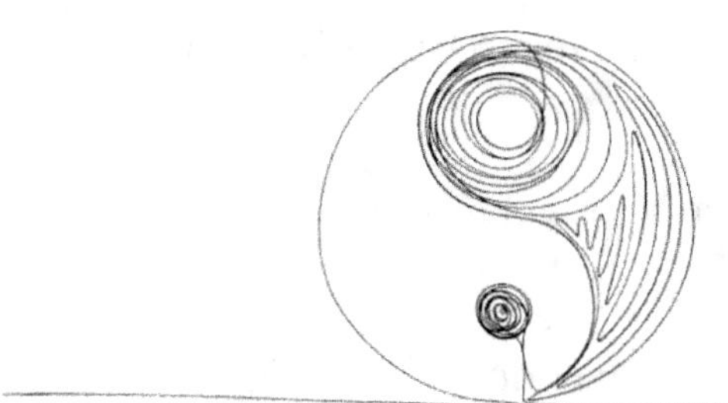

The mirror soul

Our spirits, once united, now split in two,

Birthdays shared on the 22nd, a truth I cling to.

The sum of four in the realm of spirits above,

Symbolizing unconditional love.

Reuniting, we'd soar like doves at night.

Bound by destiny, guided by light.

From Yin to yang, together, we create harmony.

As I am your Katara to Aang,

Fire and air, merging in a cosmic pang,

Our union echoes the of creation's big bang.

The notebook that was stolen

Our love tale is still being written under the stars' light.

Down on Earth, our pens align, tracing its flight.

In celestial dance, our story takes place,

A cosmic journey, bound by time and space.

Lost without you

You are there again in my dream,
I am not sure, if it's real or if it's a scheme.
The way I feel, I'm not sure if it's what it seems.
But I feel something.
Something extraordinary; it's a bit scary.
I'm not sure if what I feel is real; it's starting to
make me wary.
I'm wary if I'm going insane because the way I
feel can't be explained.
It's something unreal; it's passionate, but I'm
not sure why.
Why does it leave me wanting to know more?
About this connection.
It got me up all night thinking, could this be
destined?
Since we met once before, living two different
lives.
Thinking about you naturally gets me high.
High vibrations are what I feel; the heart
chakra is completely open, and I know that God
is holding.
You back so I can heal.
But it's not fair for me not to have you; it's like
I lost someone that I've once had, like a kill.
I am extremely passionate about something
that is unknown, like a thrill.

No more Fillers

I started to become more natural.

Because when we meet again,

I want you to see no blind spots.

I am coming to you as me,

I do not want this love to flee.

I will take the lead with authenticity.

To love

To being whole

& not half

It is a better feeling

Knowing you have all of

you.

-Jocelyn

Love is sacred

It has to be found from inside

In order for you to meet the other half

Who will show you the work you provided.

-Jocelyn

Connecting through sound

Every love song I felt deeply
Turned into you.
The music I felt through my soul,
It got deeper, the thought.
Dazed out sometimes, imagining us,
Not wanting the music to stop.

Addictions I learned were true

Limerence,
Everyone before you- that's what I felt,
Never true love,
Just fighting loneliness.
Avoiding facing the feeling,
I distracted myself until I was hit.
The realization became so real.
My whole life, I pretended simply for
amusement.
Walking unconsciously into the world,
Because I wanted to ignore what was
already coming.
Healing,
It isn't always fun.
It is something we must learn.
If we want to grow,
I'm learning as I go.

Best friend you claim

I remember, in a dream,
One of the early times, we met.
We had such a joyful dynamic.
The moment we shared, I will never forget.
Until someone came in and shot you in the
back.
It's a dream, so I knew it was symbolic.
Later, I was filled with grief.
Yes, I am still in the dream.
I found you standing right across from me.
Yes, right there.
I pretend not to see you.
I believed you were dead.
You asked if I could see you.
I ignored you instead.
You spoke again.
And of course, I said yes.
You were relieved.
I was in disbelief.
I asked who you were to me.
You said you were my best friend.
You left with a smile.
I trust your word.
Don't give me crap when I see you,
Talking about that is absurd.

Till we meet again,
Let those words hold our bond.

Call me Crazy

It feels weird to love someone.
So much, yet not to get a response.
It's hard to know what you want,
The feelings aren't mutual.
You leave me feeling desperate.
Or that is just how I see myself,
And you're reflecting.
Then I need to let go.
Because honestly, this doesn't look like
we're connecting.

Golden Hour of you

It was because of that part.

Our part was my favorite.

& still is to this day.

I want to do it again.

One day, when we understand

What we feel,

And that what we have is real.

Until divine timing.

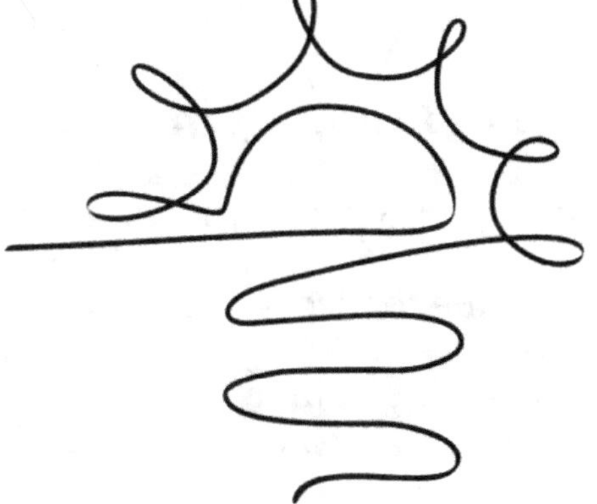

Lost myself in you

I wanted your love more than my own.

You ripped me to pieces, then left me alone.

I hated you at one point and wanted you to go away.

With mixed emotions, love comes and goes.

Your absence only made me long for your presence each day.

What I felt off memory

I remember feeling your first heartbreak.

Your energy was so sad that I wanted to take away the ache.

At this time, I was hurting and going through my own pain.

It was crazy that we were hurting at the same time, in a different place.

I was hurt because I was lost in life.

You were hurt that you lost the love that you were going to make your wife.

Yet in our shared pain, we found a bond.

Be bold

Make sure you take control.

The best is for you to

Let go.

-Jocelyn

Trust Broken Our Love has Sunken

The day I connected with your higher self,

He revealed a message I never wanted to hear.

Instantly, it brought me to tears.

He showed me a ring,

But I knew it wasn't for me because we haven't
spoken in years.

When you propose to someone else, my heart
shatters

My heart broke; I thought death was near.

In that moment, I realized our love was a
dream.

Fading away, like a whisper in the stream.

Lessons through Understanding

Learning in this connection

I hold no control

God taught me to let go.

& surrender to the flow.

Listened to every tarot reader

Telling me you will come back

Left me an illusion.

That left me insane and obsessed.

Taking my power back

There were many pieces in me that I lacked.

On this healing journey,

Self-control is the route to growth.

Thinking of you

This isn't normal; it's obsessive.

Thoughts and feelings shouldn't be possessive.

You're so far away, yet close to my heart.

Who are you? The honest answer is that I don't know where to start.

Let go, let go, let go, but I can't.

I'm pretty good at moving on, but this thought I can't transplant.

The moment I try to forget, thoughts cloud backup,

As if I erased something and then clicked undo, my thoughts were disrupted.

I remain single for the first time.

Because I've never felt this before, it's not a crime.

Isn't that crazy? I'd rather have you or none.

I've never been the type to hold on this long, but you're the one.

You have something over me; this is beyond love's hold.

Though I barely got a glimpse of you, I'm sold.

It doesn't matter who you truly are.

I want whatever comes with you, near or far.

Good or bad, happy or sad,

Anger or glad, every emotion you have.

I'll take every broken piece and try to understand.

I'll cherish every happy moment.

One thing about me is that I'm determined; I won't give up.

If you don't, I'll keep my chin up.

Don't let go; understand what you feel.

Take time to heal.

It's okay to feel, because whatever you feel, I also feel.

We're connected; our emotions seal the deal.

It's not easy, but I've done it before.

 I know you're capable; we'll open a new door.

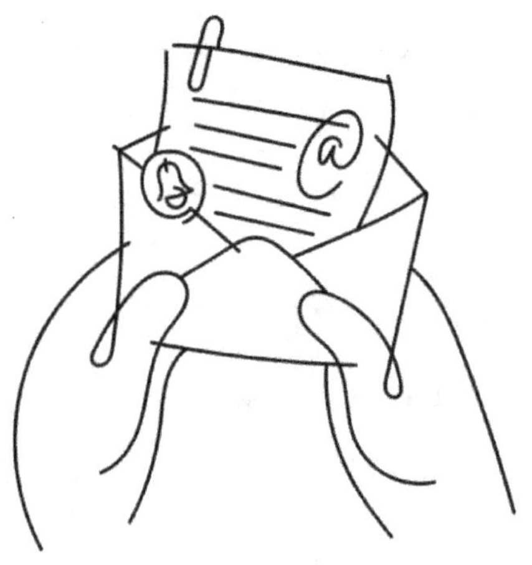

Not Bold Enough

Through emails shared, feelings confessed,
But beliefs kept us distanced, stressed.
Yet fate intervened; in class we'd meet,
Eight years on, you still make my heart feel so
sweet.

The Map of the Journey

At the beginning of the journey, I was
yearning.
In the middle, lost and depressed,
Yet, no one checked on my well-being.
My emotions fluctuated; up and down
they went.
I truly lost my so-called identity down
the road.
Fall into a deep, dark hole.
But a burst of light and hope of love
within my heart,
Propelled me towards a new beginning,
a fresh start.
Well, in the end, I can say it's getting
better.
No true journey is ever truly over.
It's just growth down the line.
New parts of you are constantly being
discovered.

Peace to Mind

Drawn to you deeply,
I've failed to connect with anyone else so
profoundly.
The bond we share seems unique.
Yet, I don't wish to intrude.
But clarity on your feelings would allow me
to move forward.
A direct response is all I seek.
So, you may proceed with your life without
hindrance.
Rest assured, I'll respect your wishes and
retreat.
Just convey if you wish to sever ties
completely.
I'll comprehend and depart without a trace.
I understand that what I felt may have been
misplaced.
This chapter was merely a charade.
But closure would grant peace to my
distraught state.
Your response would ease the torment
within.
Ending this tumult and bringing sanity
back in.
Thank you,
Mr. No Name.

Hey Barbie

I once aspired to be perfect for you,
but I learned I crossed a line, consumed
by obsession.
In my quest to please, I shed my
identity, too.
Never say never, for I sacrificed myself
for you.
But you couldn't care less if I hadn't.
Thanks for painting my love as a
delusion.
I refuse to return to my self-hate place.
Forget me, forget us.
What we lack is truth.

      Shedding old parts of me.

"On the limb"

I never felt so close.

To someone through a TV screen

It's like Shirley gets me.

Drawn to someone like you knew them before.

Things are holding you back from becoming
something more.

Wanting to understand things deeper

The coincidence becomes creepier.

Wanting the other person to be happy

Understanding that happiness resides within
you

Can leave you feeling lost at your core,

Leaving your heart torn.

I forgot to remove my thorns.

Mr. Avoidant

Love with no limitations,

You wouldn't know what to do with that.

You fear it,

So, you avoid it and run from it.

I'm here to help you overcome it,

Learn from it,

Fix the broken pieces that you destroyed,

Heal the hurt that you have been avoiding.

Feel the Emotion

Hurt and pain,

The feeling of it isn't the same.

I began to become numb to your pain.
I felt like you hadn't listened to me.
It made me feel like dirt.
Not the dry one,
The wet,
Knowing it will stick to your shoes,
But you don't clean them; you ignore them and just
forget.
Until they dry and you realize you'd rather get new
ones instead,

You want a clean slate,
The one you don't have to think about,
The one you can easily eliminate.
You probably forgot all about them the next day.
Cleared from your mind completely.
Eliminate.

Dream Spell

We connect through the astral, but never through
the physical.

I wonder if this is real or if I am delusional.

I met you in real life, but how in this realm?

Have I forgotten something? Are they dropping
new gems?

Your presence makes me happy, but only in the 5D.

The first dream I shared with you sparked my
awakening.

I could never forget how I almost caved when a kiss
came in.

My feelings have never gotten this far.

It's like we're two in one, like a pair?

I love you with all my heart.

It's never going to change, no matter how far apart
we are.

To the flame who sparks light into my spirit

Denying is lying

I hate that I'm stuck on you,
While you live your best life,
I bet you don't have a clue.
You stabbed my heart with a knife.
My body is frozen and completely blue.
I found out you are married with a wife.
What did I ever do to hurt you?
I must give up on you this time.
Knowing you, this isn't anything new.
I wanted to call you, my boo.
While you have me out here looking like a fool,
Good luck to you!
In your new love,
I hope you get everything you ever dreamed of.

Just a random girl with feelings.

About you

I no longer want to be your other half.

Until you learn to love yourself whole

Because without you complete

This relationship will always be a defeat.

You are more important than anything.

You need to learn that you are not a peasant
and that your value is much more like that of a
king.

Not the one who cares about the bling.

The one who isn't afraid to show his willpower
as his core and build a bond within himself is
all he needs.

Stop letting people dictate your life and put
aside your pride.

Learn to love yourself when others doubt you
and want you to lie.

Stop the fake smile. I see straight through your
clever eyes.

You act like you're perfect when you know
you're hurting.

But you have a chance to heal. Let your
emotions run through you freely.

I'll be on the other side, ready to hold you
dearly.

But I don't want your act, petty and pretend.

I want your mask off; I want you to reveal your
true self at the end.

So, until then, I will write until you realize I'm
not giving up but neither giving in.

We know who you really want to become, and
I'll be waiting for him to behold his throne.

My love for you will always be the truth.

Only if you knew

Your incomplete half.

Broken pieces and promises

You do anything for them and nothing for
yourself.

That's the same feeling I felt for you.

But I wanted you to put your love on the line
for me.

Die for me.

But you made sure to say goodbye to me.

Choose someone else and run and hide from
me.

My heart shattered to know you would lie to
me.

Yet in the ruins of trust, I found strength to
rise.

To mend my broken spirit and seek love that
flies.

Though your departure stung, it set my spirit
free.

To find someone who cherishes the love they
offer me.

Enchanted With My Love

I never got the chance to give up on love.

I found out what I was truly made of.

God speaks to me, and I'm learning to listen.

I changed my life.

I can't believe I didn't get defeated.

I started meditating and started to receive it.

The frequency of love is strong and beautiful; you better believe it.

I found out the power is stored within

Once you master it, nobody can touch you; they must knock before they get in.

Embrace it truly and say I receive it.

To Love

Hugs and Kisses

Hugs for knowing I won't let go until you let me
know this isn't what you want.

You had so many times to express that I'm not the
girl you have in mind.

A simple no would be really kind.

Kisses are what I'll do if you say goodbye.

I will let go of you and move on to the next one,
who is on my highest timeline.

I can't wait forever for someone to get it together.

We will meet again in another lifetime.

Maybe even as friends and have an unbreakable
bond.

This life continues to go on.

Until then

Xoxo

Where is my Flowers

I wanted you to give me my flowers.

I have been waiting for hours.

For you to show up

And not be a coward.

My apologies

I mean for you to come on.

I have been waiting for hours.

Not trying to be sour

I understand it takes time to get into your power.

Soon you will go through a tower.

Which is the transition from all you know

Something that you must encounter

For you to let go,

Emotions will finally flow. It will be wet, like a shower.

Until then, I'll be waiting for you with my flowers.

Higher Self and You

If I'm being honest,
I'm going to tell you the truth.
I don't think I've been connecting with you.
I believe your Higher Self has played a huge role in
my life.
I don't think you truly have care for me in mind.
I wouldn't be surprised if you didn't know I existed
I remember I approached you, and you wouldn't
even look at me; you completely ignored my
presence.
As if I weren't even there,
Maybe that moment held significance.
Maybe you were showing me what I do to myself.
It hits differently when it's coming from someone
else.
But damn, you didn't even ask me if I needed help.
You never really give me advice or even ask me
about my life.
You truly avoid me all the time.
You don't even know what I am truly like.
Because you avoid me at all costs.
Theres two sides of you I see
I wish you would listen to your higher self
So, you can see the other side of you I also see
Connecting to your self is a beautiful thing.

Best believe…

Those Sad Eyes

Yearning, yet crying inside
The love I shared with you was only genuine.
I cared about you and kept you close, like a mother
penguin.
I never wanted to let you go,
But the love wasn't reciprocated.
And you have no problem letting me know.
Dust me off like nothing,
Moved on to the next,
I mean, what can I expect?
Avoidant attachment,
You couldn't care less.

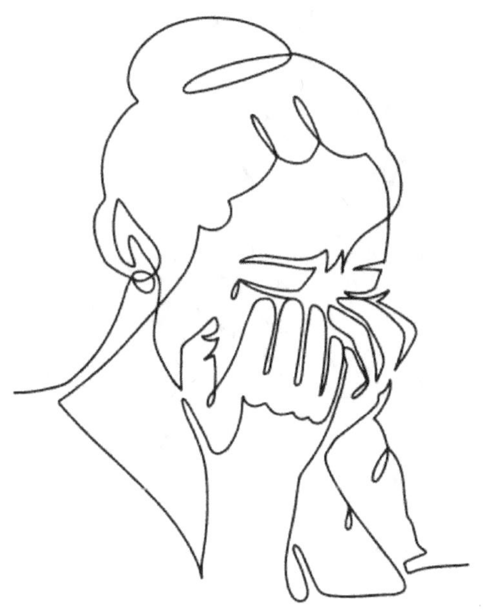

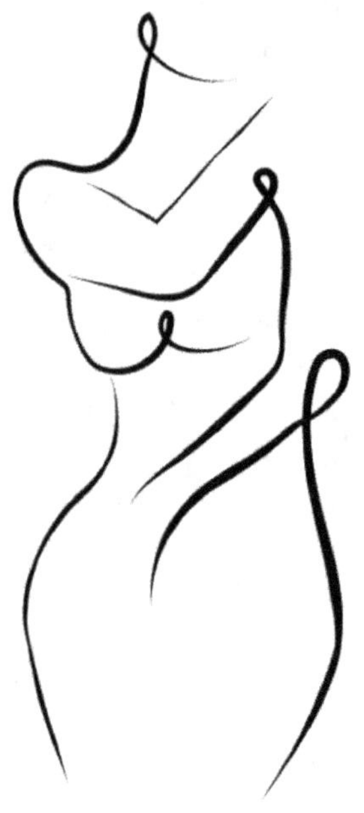

Celibacy

I have been celibate for a long time now.

I learned I'm not good with the quick run around.

I don't want someone on my body for a test drive,

I want to make love with the love of my life.

We connect so deeply, it's not just sex.

What we feel is a bond forming as I open my legs.

Eyes locked, as you read the notes in my head.

As we start to moan, we release dopamine.

I'm talking about real love, not some sex scene.

Oxytocin is what you release when you're feeling
pleased.

Love particles all over the room.

Expressing love through the body and while the
spirits reunite.

Game over

Once you got married,
That put the icing on the cake.
You officially maximized my level of heartbreak.
I was so hurt that I fell to my knees and couldn't
move.
My body was only able to shake.
Lost for words
I thought we could make it work.
I felt so insecure.
Disgusted
Misled
Felt insane
The only thing I could feel was that my body was
completely numb and filled with pain.
Your higher self-heard my cry.
I wanted even him to go because
Everything I knew from there was a lie.
In that moment, I never wanted anyone to love me.
I truly wanted to die
But instead of that, all I could do was cry.
Goodbye.

Sexuality Is Part of My Identity

Ashamed of my body, Thanks to all the name-calling.

 Not feeling worthy to even feel, in this sick world we live in. Too many rules that take away the thrill, learning to express my sexuality fully. Touches, skin, and feelings I dare someone to tell me otherwise. With audacity, I am a free spirit, exploring myself, but here's the truth:

I accept me, and that's what matters.

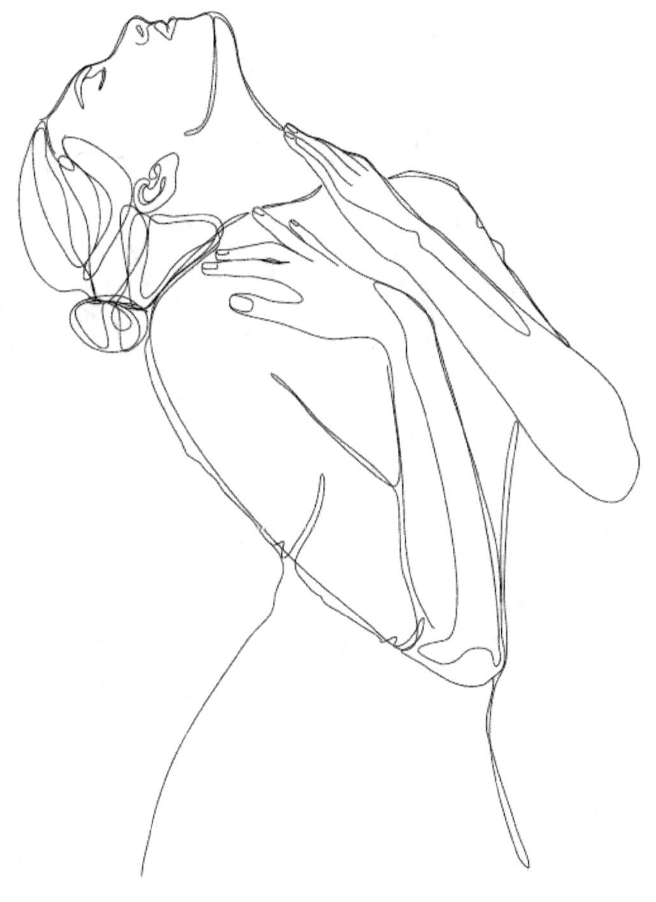

Violet Came In and gave me light

I save Violet for her to save me.

With an owner who had no place to be found

She was helpless and was going to put her down.

I asked God thirty seconds early to give me the dog that needed to be found.

I was going to choose a boy, but received a girl

She has helped me stay stable in this world.

The sweetest spirit and the kindest heart

I am learning love through an animal.

Believe me, they are very smart.

Love to my ViVi

Recovery to Restart

I do good.

Then Bad

One day, I'll be fully happy.

Then Sad

Work hard

To fall

I wish my life would do a 360.

Right about now

Not able to stay stable

I guess I'm enabled.

About me

I know you're probably thinking I'm wild.

Someone with so many emotions,
Who can hardly express them out loud,
Switching them up as quickly as the snap of a pen.

Once I started to learn to write,
That's when the journey truly began.
Focused on mastering these energies,
It hasn't been so easy.
Finally focusing on me,
Taking time to become one,
With my mind, spirit, and body.

Never letting anyone have that much control,
It took a minute to get over it.
My mind took many turns and reached a toll.
Focused on the outcome,
I forgot to enjoy the moment.
Now it's here, and as I have flashbacks of the past,
I can finally accept that it happened.

And in order for me to grow,
No more looking at it as a time I was mentally slow,
Because now I have reached a love that is
unconditional.
The parts I discovered have a significant glow.
I'm finally ready to shine.
I'm ready to let it show.

P.S. The side of me that has always been hidden.

Forgive

I must be okay.

If we never cross paths again,

Yes, you broke my heart.

I wanted you to love me in the dark.

But I have now created light.

Through the hurt and pain

Forgiveness is what I will do now.

I learned the best way to love.

Is to understand, and I do

Thank you for being my guide.

To self.

Race to Save Face

I never knew if you'd truly approve,

Of whom I am.

Because I'm of a different race, not like you.

Skin tones diverge, but hearts beat the same

rhythm divine.

Dreams That Stream from telepathy

I have had at least 30 dreams about you at night.

Back-to-back now, someone tells me this is crazy because that doesn't seem right.

You have told me about your issues stimming from childhood; nobody would know you're hurting inside.

There are times when you're smiling, and you feel lonely all the time.

You just want to be loved but must please to make things right.

You have an issue that you learn to keep buried to make others feel nice.

You love so hard, but no one ever truly notices you save face, so you don't get an ugly look because you're not the type that really wants to put up a fight.

You have such a sweetheart, but your insecurities are strong. Tell me if I'm not right.

I know you like a book because I understand

I pray you grow into a very strong confident man.

You just want real love, and now that I can truly understand.

The Flower That Blossomed

I was so scared to get out of the ground.

Nobody ever talks to me. Nobody ever came around.

I wanted to bloom but saw no sunlight.

Not enough water to keep me satisfied

Losing touch with my identity

I lost my mind and thought I was going insane.

Being walked on by others

Nobody stopped by to make sure I was watered

I feel a root pushing me down inside.

Telling me to go and not hide

The feeling was a root that felt like mine.

I don't think it is ready; I could feel its love being applied to mine.

I felt the need to show the world I am not ready to die.

Or even be buried alive.

I was ready to shine

Through patience and strength

I sprouted to the full length. People noticed the change and felt my love shine through the rain.

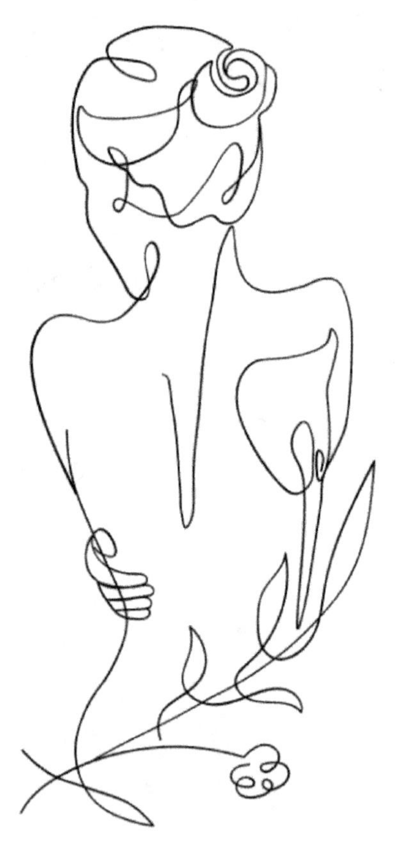

Naked Hair

Went natural

Talking about my hair

When I was younger,

I was extremely insecure, but no one cared

I always knew I was going to lead this connection
with love.

& by doing that, I had to undo all the self-hatred I
was taught.

I want you to see my imperfections.

& naturalness with only beauty

Coming to your thought

Here's to purified.

Butterflies mean transformation

I keep seeing yellow butterflies

Yellow represents willpower

But I'm stuck on you, and I

I'm not sure how to get over this soul tie.

But the butterflies won't stop showing me yellow.

They're putting up a fight for me to reunite.

with myself

my confidence

& power

Here's to the butterflies who have guided me to my own love path, to proceeding from yellow to green.

If you understand colors, you know what I mean.

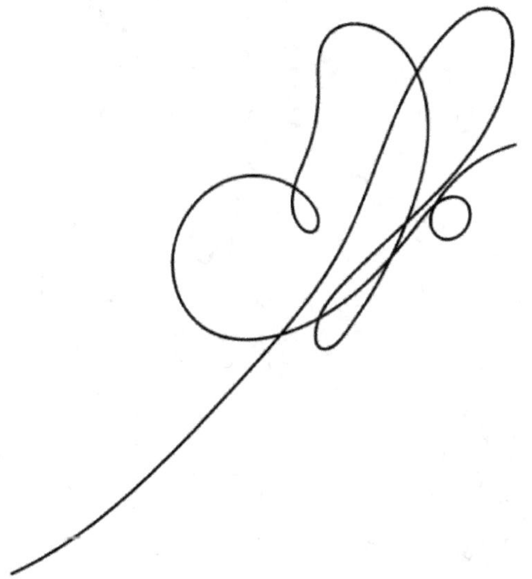

Even the bird wants me to find the meaning of love

Even the birds want me to find love.

Flying around me, chirping the most beautiful sound

Through frequency, I can tell they don't want me to give up.

Getting so close, I feel they want to give me a hug.

One guy was spying on me, and they started to hit him with their beak.

I guess that's their way of saying, Keep your guard up.

Thank you, birds, for watching over me.

You won't read this, but I'm letting the world know you are loved.

Chirp Chirp

Forbidden Love

I understand you want people to see you as a
righteous man.
You told me what you were afraid of.
You never wanted to be ashamed of
Your beliefs are what's keeping you stagnant.
Not wanting your parents to know you might want
something different.
So, you stick to what you know.
To keep a good look
But inside, you're burning to be released.
From the hurt and pain
You want it to cease.
Rather, make others happy
Instead of finding your peace,
A true lover's boy with no way out
Hurting real deep.
I'm sorry you have to go through this.
I believe you are learning a lesson.
Soon you will teach.
That choosing others over you
It will always be a battle because you are stuck in
between.
Of lovin yourself or seeing others flee
The choice is yours.
A word of advice is just to have faith and believe.

Cycle of Healing

What does real healing look like?
It Isn't perfection
It isn't you going straight towards the destine.
It's getting confused and lost along the way.
Losing sight of what you thought was great
Taking time to unravel the pain.
Understanding it and letting it go will allow you to grow.
Because you no longer want the pain to interfere with your present and who you are becoming.
You're learning to leave it all behind as if it isn't nothing
I never said you will forget it but you release it, so it doesn't affect you
No one can tease it.

Welcome to the world newborn.

Soul baby soul

You're an electric, magnetic beam.

It's hard for negativity to intervene.

When you are at a high vibration

Concentrating on the things you lack.

Keep focusing on the things that bring you peace.

Never lose track of things that put your mind at

ease.

The trusting process

The motivation of you
I sit here in the car, wondering how I got this far.
The progression that had to happen for me to keep
myself up to par
Most would say it's easy, but for me, it took time to
love me in the dark.
It took time to realize that I was the spark.
Many nights of crying in the car
Plenty of weeks of trying to drown
myself at the bar.
Realizing I can't drown in my sorrows.

Tap into myself now; I am better, and the love
frequency follows.

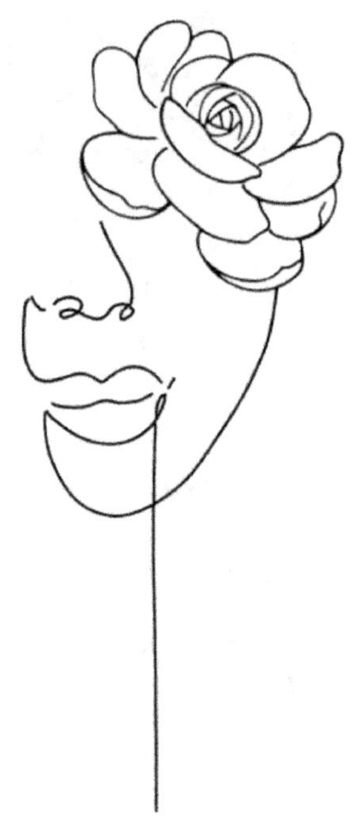

Take Notes

As I sit her tipsy, I realize the dark has taught me
so much.
It's a beautiful curse that was scary to face.
Holding on to hurt will never make you great, you
will always remain the same.
I'm not just good, and I'm not all bad.
Some days I can be happy but also sad.
Duality of life is real you need a balance for you to
heal.
The dark has to be brought to light.
It won't be easy to see, but that's ok.
Understanding yourself will make you the master of
your own mind.

Golden Hour of Us

The sun is out and bright,
WInd flowing from left to right, connected to the
breeze,
Arms wide open, wishing I could jump into your arms
with ease.

Imagination is where I live, in my head,
While you rent the place out for a year now,
Eviction isn't a choice, so I guess I can say you're stuck
with me,
Not in order, but my mind can drift just as far apart as
we are.

I want to touch you,
Honestly, in many ways,
I want to tickle you to see you laugh and smile,
I want to look at you and touch your face to admire
your beautiful sculpture.

Then kiss you and hold it until we connect to our hearts,
And I want to stare into your eyes after to remind you
that our love is that deep,
That the kiss is the physical way for us to connect, but
our eyes are what hold us spiritually.
I love you both ways, completely,
Until divine timing.

Reminder!

They never said self-love would be easy. It doesn't matter how you look because you could be cute on the outside but internally feel horrible. So, the work must be done internally. Plus, everyone has their own perspective on why they neglect themselves, depending on how they were raised, people's influence, media influence, and society standards. But it's so important that you learn to understand the internal you because that reflects your personality, body, and perspective. It's not easy, but it takes time. Noticing your flaws yourself, seeing the patterns that repeat, what you're lacking in your worth – the real healing just starts with noticing. There's no rush or finish line to this journey. Once you realize your worth, it gets scary how much you want to spend time with yourself, enjoy your own presence, and just be happy no matter what that is, doing or saying. Remember we all have light within us. It's time that we stop chasing the light and learn to embrace it.

I love you

P.s Jocelyn Shade